EAT LIKE BOOK SERIE

Eat Like a Local- Sarasota: Sarasota Florida Food Guide

I have lived in the Sarasota area since 1998 and learned about many great places that I want to try. –Conoal

Eat Like a Local: Connecticut: Connecticut Food Guide

This a great guide to try different places in Connecticut to eat. Can't wait to try them all! The author is awesome to explore and try all these different foods/drinks. There are places I didn't know they existed until I got this book and I am a CT resident myself! –Caroline J. H.

Eat Like a Local: Las Vegas: Las Vegas Nevada Food Guide

Perfect food guide for any tourist traveling to Vegas or any local looking to go outside their comfort zone! – TheBondes

Eat Like a Local-Jacksonville: Jacksonville Florida Food Guide

Loved the recommendations. Great book from someone who knows their way around Jacksonville. –Anonymous

Eat Like a Local- Costa Brava: Costa Brava Spain Food Guide

The book was very well written. Visited a few of the restaurants in the book, they were great! Sylvia V.

Eat Like a Local-Sacramento: Sacramento California Food Guide

As a native of Sacramento, Emerald's book touches on some of our areas premier spots for food and fun. She skims the surface of what Sacramento has to offer recommending locations in historical, popular areas where even more jewels can be found. –Katherine G.

EAT LIKE A LOCAL- MÁLAGA

Málaga Spain Food Guide

Melissa Joy Bitz

Eat Like a Local- Málaga Copyright © 2022 by CZYK Publishing LLC. All Rights Reserved.

All rights reserved. No part of this book may be reproduced in any form or by any electronic or mechanical means including information storage and retrieval systems, without permission in writing from the author. The only exception is by a reviewer, who may quote short excerpts in a review.

The statements in this book are of the authors and may not be the views of CZYK Publishing.

Cover designed by: Lisa Rusczyk Ed. D.

CZYK Publishing Since 2011.
CZYKPublishing.com
Eat Like a Local

Mill Hall, PA
All rights reserved.
ISBN: 9798359102940

EAT
Like A Local

BOOK DESCRIPTION

Are you excited about planning your next trip? Do you want an edible experience? Would you like some culinary guidance from a local? If you answered yes to any of these questions, then this Eat Like a Local book is for you. Eat Like a Local - Málaga, Spain by author Melissa Joy Bitz offers the inside scoop on some of the best gastronomic experiences Málaga has to offer. Culinary tourism is an important aspect of any travel experience. Food has the ability to tell you a story of a destination, its landscapes, and culture on a single plate. Most food guides tell you how to eat like a tourist. Although there is nothing wrong with that, as part of the Eat Like a Local series, this book will give you a food guide from someone who has lived at your next culinary destination.

In these pages, you will discover advice on having a unique edible experience. This book will not tell you exact addresses or hours but instead will give you excitement and knowledge of food and drinks from a local that you may not find in other travel food guides.

Eat like a local. Slow down, stay in one place, and get to know the food, people, and culture. By the time you finish this book, you will be eager and prepared to travel to your next culinary destination.

OUR STORY

Traveling has always been a passion of the creator of the Eat Like a Local book series. During Lisa's travels in Malta, instead of tasting what the city offered, she ate at a large fast-food chain. However, she realized that her traveling experience would have been more fulfilling if she had experienced the best of local cuisines. Most would agree that food is one of the most important aspects of a culture. Through her travels, Lisa learned how much locals had to share with tourists, especially about food. Lisa created the Eat Like a Local book series to help connect people with locals which she discovered is a topic that locals are very passionate about sharing. So please join me and: Eat, drink, and explore like a local.

TABLE OF CONTENTS

Eat Like a Local-
Book Series Reviews
BOOK DESCRIPTION
OUR STORY
TABLE OF CONTENTS
DEDICATION
ABOUT THE AUTHOR
HOW TO USE THIS BOOK
FROM THE PUBLISHER

1. A tip tip
2. Careful with
closing days
3. What about breakfast?
4. Speaking of breakfast…how to order coffee in Málaga
5. So long Starbucks
6. Fancy a nice cuppa?
7. Girls just wanna have brunch
8. Everyday bakery treats
9. Can you take the heat? Uh, I mean..grease?
10. Lunch Time Warp
11. The best lunchtime value
12. When in Spain, thou shalt "tapear"!
13. What´s that smoke coming from the beach?

14. Singing for your tapas
15. Little fish, little fish
16. Don´t be a landlubber
17. Muy Malaguita
18. Humble pie
19. Somewhere, beyond the sea…somewhere waiting for me…
20. Little gems
21. Touristy havens
22. Cheap eats
23. Get your healthy on!
24. Fancy Schmancy
25. No meat? No problem!
26. Málaga multi-culti
27. Mexican hat dance
28. From the Far East
29. Dolce Vittoria
30. Street food
31. Late night eats
32. Italy´s got nothing on us!
33. Thank you, Spaniards, for the chocolate
34. Cocktails al fresco with a bird´s eye view
35. Málaga wine
36. The weekend ritual of vermouth
37. Creative Cocktailery
38. Where everybody knows your name

39. The alchemy of wine
40. A taste of history
41. Authentic market atmosphere
42. The English Cut
43. If your blood runs green
44. A pinch of spice in paradise
45. Aperitif, anyone?
46. Festival Food
47. Chestnuts a´ roasting
48. Food fairs with flair
49. Christmas time, oh Christmas time
50. El Pimpi legacy

Other Resources:

READ OTHER BOOKS BY
CZYK PUBLISHING

DEDICATION

I dedicate this book to my one-and-only big sis, Holly. You have been my strong protector and advocate. And you have also shown me the strength of a deeply caring and tender heart. Together we´re unstoppable, babe. See you on the next adventure!

ABOUT THE AUTHOR

Melissa was born in Colorado in the western United States. She is a lover of learning, mastery, and linguistics. By college, she discovered that she was born to explore, live, love, and "eat the world" (as they say in Spanish). Toting her summa cum laude Master´s degree hot off the press, she moved to Spain and became a teacher of English and a student of life. After 18 years of the unique food, rich culture, and abundant rain of Asturias, she decided to head due south to the balmy Mediterranean of Málaga where she now soaks up its unique food, rich culture, and abundant sun.

HOW TO USE THIS BOOK

The goal of this book is to help culinary travelers either dream or experience different edible experiences by providing opinions from a local. The author has made suggestions based on their own knowledge. Please do your own research before traveling to the area in case the suggested locations are unavailable.

Travel Advisories: As a first step in planning any trip abroad, check the Travel Advisories for your intended destination.
https://travel.state.gov/content/travel/en/traveladvisories/traveladvisories.html

FROM THE PUBLISHER

Traveling can be one of the most important parts of a person's life. The anticipation and memories that you have are some of the best. As a publisher of the *Eat Like a Local*, Greater Than a Tourist, as well as the popular *50 Things to Know* book series, we strive to help you learn about new places, spark your imagination, and inspire you. Wherever you are and whatever you do I wish you safe, fun, and inspiring travel.

Lisa Rusczyk Ed. D.
CZYK Publishing

Eat Like a Local

Ask not what you can do for your country. Ask what's for lunch.

~Orson Welles

When I lived in America, even with the so-called SAD (Standard American Diet), I didn't feel as if I ate badly. Neither was I a "bon-vivant" around food in those days. I didn't overindulge or eat too many sweets, drink too much, or indulge in too many high-carb foods. For me, food was food. Yes, it was something you could enjoy and maybe even savor. But after living in Spain for the last 19 years, I now know that I didn't really eat to a higher standard either because I didn't really know that such a thing existed.

In Spain, there is more of a preoccupation with the quality of the food you are eating. Get to know some Spaniards and you'll often hear conversations about where it comes from, how it is raised, whether it is fresh or frozen, and how it is prepared (either correctly or incorrectly of course!). In Asturias, It was impressed on me early on that the most rustic-looking places with a granny in the kitchen would most likely have the tastiest dishes. These were often homes where the ground floor was a dining room with 5 or 6 small tables while the upstairs was the living quarters of the owners and their family. These were the best places for a 3-hour Sunday lunch with friends, or to shake off the sand and sun after a perfect day at the beach.

In Málaga, the focus on quality and variety (and the beach) is also noticeable, but with added flexibility for the more robust tourist industry. The warmer climate naturally influences the local fare and culinary tendencies. Cooling gazpacho is a must-have for me nowadays. But what really makes me feel as if I´m living and dining in an extraordinary place is how a "typical" food can have a deeply-woven history behind it. On a visit to Málaga´s municipal museum, I was surprised to find some paintings of ladies dressed in 19th-century fashion, gathered together on the beach with fish roasting on spits. I immediately recognized the famous "espeto," the skewered sardines roasted over embers (see Tip 13) that you still see today at the beachfront "chiringuitos". And this is just a slight hop into the past! Phoenician fishermen also had the custom of cooking their catch over open fires on these same shores some 2,800 years ago. How´s that for tradition!

Eat Like a Local

As always, whatever gastronomical adventures you choose, please be sure to check restaurant hours, make reservations if necessary, and research any other particulars you may wish to know beforehand. I have only offered my own experience in these pages but yours will be unique. ¡Que disfruten de su estancia!

Málaga
Spain

Malaga Spain Climate

	High	Low
January	62	46
February	64	47
March	67	49
April	70	52
May	76	57
June	82	64
July	87	68
August	87	70
September	83	68
October	75	59
November	68	52
December	63	47

GreaterThanaTourist.com

Temperatures are in Fahrenheit degrees.
Source: NOAA

Eat Like a Local

Photographer: Melissa Joy Bitz

1. A TIP TIP

Wherever you are from in the world, there are norms around tipping. Where I come from, the rule is 15% of the bill, but 20% is better. Even after many years in Spain, I can still witness this conditioning in myself. One day at the hairdresser´s, I attempted to leave a 20% tip only to get my €5 bill pushed right back into my hand by my well-meaning hair stylist! Here in Spain, it´s not a percentage of the bill, but more like a few extra coins you leave on the table for good will. So I suggest striking a middle ground. I try to add a bit more than a typical tip but I never calculate the tip based on my internal "20% rule." For example, for a €20 meal, I might leave around €2. If you book a larger group at a restaurant, they will most likely add a gratuity charge to the bill automatically.

2. CAREFUL WITH CLOSING DAYS

In the hospitality industry in Spain, it is very common for bars, restaurants, and cafés to choose a weekday as their closing day of rest for employees. I find that Monday and Tuesday are the most common days that you might rock up and find it locked up. Although Sunday is a good day for business, there are still many places that respect rest and family time for their employees. Therefore, there will be some places closed on Sundays as well. Just make sure and fire up your Google search and confirm before you head out so you won't be disappointed.

3. WHAT ABOUT BREAKFAST?

Is breakfast really the most important meal of the day? Well…not really. Not in Spain anyway. Of course this doesn't mean that people just skip it but a typical local "desayuno" is quite simple. Coffee? Essential. Some kind of bread or roll? Essential. Perhaps a little glass of orange juice? Sure. And that's about it! If you want to blend in with the locals, I would suggest stepping out of your normal brekky routine to try a "pitufo" (translated as "smurf") which is a toasted piece of traditional bread ("mollete") with a variety of toppings like tomato, olive oil, jam, butter, cheese, or other combinations. On the other hand, if you're set on doing a big breakfast American style, you can always visit La Desayunería where you can find dozens of kinds of pancakes, breakfast platters, smoothies, and lots of other treats. Just make sure you've got room for muchas calorías!

4. SPEAKING OF BREAKFAST...HOW TO ORDER COFFEE IN MÁLAGA

Not long after moving to Málaga, I attended a morning get-together with several ladies at a local café. Planning to order a simple, "café con leche," I soon found myself quite confused as each one spoke to the waiter using a "lingo" I´d never heard before! It turns out that there are no less than 8 ways to order coffee depending on the proportion of milk to coffee in the cup. If you like your coffee strong and black, with no milk, it´s a "café solo." If you like it weaker and more watery, with no milk, it´s a "café americano." Adding milk makes it even more complicated! Mostly coffee with a dash of milk is a "café largo." Half coffee and half milk is a "mitad," and with just a touch more milk than a mitad is an "entrecorto". A "corto" is about ⅓ coffee, ⅔ milk. A "sombra" is about ¼ coffee, ¾ milk. And finally, a "nube" (meaning "cloud") is mostly milk with a dash of coffee. Good luck ordering! Or you could just sheepishly say, "café con leche."

5. SO LONG STARBUCKS

Ok, we all might indulge in a little Starbucks from time to time. No harm, no foul. But while in Málaga, why not give a little of your custom to a local coffee joint? After all, Europe is known to have some damn tasty coffee! Not too long ago, I discovered Delicotte. These people are coffee experts right down to having 6 ways to extract the coffee like Aeropress, Japanese Siphon, and French Press just to name a few. They clearly know their product and can advise you about what beans to buy and from what regions to give you the best nuance of flavors for home brewing. Try their "café con hielo" (iced coffee) on one of those warm Málaga days.

6. FANCY A NICE CUPPA?

If you can´t get through a day without a soothing cup of tea, Málaga has ya covered! All your tea desires will be fulfilled at La Tetería on Calle San Augustín. From their terrace, you can sip away your stress with a view of the San Augustín church and a sweet treat for comfort. There´s no lack of tea options whether it be white, black, green, red, herbal, or rooibos. Choose your tea by country if you prefer: China, Japan, India, or Taiwan. There is an extensive menu of homemade cakes and other sweet items like crepes, croissants, shakes, and smoothies. A few things that make this place extra special are their iced tea drinks (quite uncommon in Spain) and Arabic sweets. No need to flee if you´re a coffee drinker and they also have hot chocolate!

7. GIRLS JUST WANNA HAVE BRUNCH

To be clear, brunch is not really a Spanish thing. Aren't the English so clever, inventing this perfect-sounding mash-up of the words "breakfast" and "lunch"? Brunch is like saying on a lazy Sunday, "Well, I'm finally up and breakfast time has long since passed but hey, let's just have it anyway even though it's 1:00 pm." So even though it's not really a local custom, you just so happen to have the luxury of brunch in Málaga because tourism is a thing. The franchise, Brunchit is quite popular because of its varied menu and several locations in Málaga.

8. EVERYDAY BAKERY TREATS

In Spain, the baked goods found in local "panaderías" and "pastelerías" are divine. Just catch the slightest scent of freshly baked confections while walking by and you won´t be able to resist! At La Canasta, you can sample cakes and pastries galore from carrot cake to tartlets to croissants. They also have little sandwiches and a few full-size ones too if you´re in for a light lunch or snack. Try out La Flor Negra if you´re around the center. Conveniently located on Calle Lucía close to the Plaza de la Constitución, they have a selection of exquisite cakes. There are plenty of choices on their breakfast menu, or if you´re just hankering for a little something to have with your coffee.

9. CAN YOU TAKE THE HEAT? UH, I MEAN..GREASE?

Who doesn't love a plate of hot, freshly-fried churros? I confess I love them dipped in the double-thick "chocolate caliente" that they are typically served with. If you don't like hot chocolate with an almost pudding-like consistency, perhaps you should order coffee or Cola Cao instead. In Málaga, you can try the traditional "Madrileño" churros, loop-shaped ropes of fried dough with ridges (which makes them crispy). A famous churro spot for these is the aptly-named, historical Café Madrid in the center. The traditional "Malagueño" churro, on the other hand, is actually called a "tejeringo." These are rounder, smoother, and softer than the Madrileño variety. One popular venue, Tejeringo's café, can be found dotted around the city.

10. LUNCH TIME WARP

Lunchtime is sacred in Spain. Sacred and a bit later than other countries. As a foodie and a tourist, keep in mind that many of the restaurants you'll want to try do not have uninterrupted open hours. The general rule is lunch starts around 1:00 pm and goes until 4:00 pm, and I wouldn't recommend missing this precious slot and then expecting to find something delightful. By five-ish, you've missed the boat in the best places and then you'll have to wait until 9:00 pm for dinner. That being said, in a tourist capital like Málaga, there are restaurants adapted to tourist timetables so you won't go hungry either.

11. THE BEST LUNCHTIME VALUE

The "menu of the day" is an institution, not only in Spain but in several other European countries as well. Just think… the "menu du jour" in France, the "menù del giorno" in Italy, and the "menu do dia" in Portugal. This is a wonderful invention because it gives you the chance to try different typical dishes while paying around €10. What could be better? In Spain, you usually find at least four different options for each course chalked onto a slate board. First, you have the "primer plato" usually consisting of vegetables, soup, or legumes. Then there is the "segundo," which involves meat or fish, but there are often vegetarian options as well. Next comes the "postre" or dessert which can be homemade but isn´t always. Bread and a drink are also part of a "menú" but be advised that you don´t have much more than beer, house wine, or water included in the menu price. In any case, this is something both tourists and locals take advantage of and it can be a good experience if you find a menu that sounds tasty.

12. WHEN IN SPAIN, THOU SHALT "TAPEAR"!

That's "tah-pay-AR" for those of you keen on learning Spanish. You simply cannot come to Spain and not have a tapas experience. What, you ask, are tapas exactly? Basically, they are small plates of food served alongside drinks such as beer or wine. They can be as simple as a dish of local olives or as elaborate as the tapas at Kortxo - Fusion Art Restaurant. If you are open to new experiences, the more gourmet tapas will delight your taste buds with a unique combination of ingredients and flavors. These will naturally be more expensive but there is a healthy range of prices and tastes available to any visitor. For two different styles of tapas that are easy on the wallet, try La Tranca and El Tapeo de Cervantes.

13. WHAT'S THAT SMOKE COMING FROM THE BEACH?

One of the most iconic dishes of Málaga is the "espeto," sardines grilled on a cane skewer over embers stoked in an old fishing boat. Served with just sea salt and lemon, this dish is not only healthy but historical. As the story goes, King Alfonso XIII was visiting Málaga in 1885 to view the damage caused by the terrible earthquake of Christmas Day, 1884. As the King tried to sample this local curiosity using a knife and fork, he was told that they should be eaten with the hands. And they are still eaten this way of course and should you be adventurous enough to try them, there is a proper way to do it. Pick up a sardine with two hands holding the head with one hand and the tail with the other. You should see the fish starting to flake a bit. Eat the slightly flaking fish off of one side and then the other. It should come right off the bones easily. Just leave the head and tail part on the bones and move on to the next one! BTW, espetos are best in the months with no "r".

14. SINGING FOR YOUR TAPAS

If you´re up for a truly local "close contact" experience, the historical El Pimpi Florida might just be the place for you. Established in 1952 as a humble bar for fishermen to drink wine and play dominoes, now the locals and some adventurous outsiders wait in line to get into this narrow bar of about 30 square meters. Expect to order excellent seafood tapas and wine, and to be pressed together as more revelers wedge themselves into this small but joyful locale. The heart of this place is the boisterous singing of the Spanish "copla," an artistic form of popular Spanish song, which creates an energy of connectedness and "alegría." Located in the neighborhood of El Palo, the best way to get there is to take eastbound bus number 3 from the center.

15. LITTLE FISH, LITTLE FISH

In the province of Málaga, there's a local lingo around food. It's good to know some of the terms you will most certainly come across during your stay. One such term is "pescaito," pronounced "pes-cai-EE-to". This term reflects a particular affection that locals have for this dish because it's something like saying, "little fishies" instead of just "fish", "pescado" in Spanish. Native to the waters of southern Spain, these "boquerones" or anchovies are served either fried in olive oil or marinated in vinegar and oil. I like them both ways. Frying them correctly can be a little tricky, so I suggest ordering them at El Tintero or Chiringuito La Farola where they know how to prepare them to crispy perfection.

16. DON'T BE A LANDLUBBER

When visiting seafaring cultures, one must sample the seafood. As long as I've lived in Spain, I've always been able to find high-quality fish and seafood. Having grown up landlocked next to the Rocky Mountains, it didn't take me long to realize what I'd been missing. If you love fresh flavors from the sea, the diners at Los Mellizos in Soho always rave about the service as well as the quality of the "fritura," the fried dishes. Also, try Marisquería El Cateto which is a bit north of the historical center but worth the taxi ride or a long stroll. It's one of those unassuming neighborhood restaurants that doesn't look like much but stands out in quality and friendly but professional service.

17. MUY MALAGUITA

It's a really good thing to have an adventurous spirit towards new dishes and ingredients when traveling. Of course, you might not like everything you try, but you might also be surprised by a few things you didn't expect to love. In Málaga, there is a tradition of humble and simple dishes that you may be tempted to skip. But be brave, my friends! Be adventurous, give your tastebuds a chance to adjust to some more provocative flavors! If you already like the cold, tomato-based soup "gazpacho," give "ajoblanco" a try. Similarly, it is a cold soup but instead of tomatoes, it is almond-based and contains bread and garlic ("ajo") as well.

18. HUMBLE PIE

Gazpachuelo, perota, migas. These are some common traditional dish names that you might see or hear around Málaga. Being a big fan of the well-known Spanish "gazpacho", I thought "gazpachuelo" had to be something similar. I soon found out otherwise. The unusual gazpachuelo, which became a staple for families of modest means, is the product of scrappy fishermen who used what they had around to fill out their dish and to fill their bellies. It is based in fish broth with homemade mayonnaise and potatoes but apparently, there are as many variations of this dish as there are families. The spicy broth kept a fisherman warm while encouraging him to drink more wine at the local bars and cafés.

19. SOMEWHERE, BEYOND THE SEA…SOMEWHERE WAITING FOR ME…

I don´t know if your lover stands on golden sands but in the "chiringuitos" is where you can watch the ships as they go sailin´. The word "chiringuito" (pronounced "cheer-ing-GHEE-toe") usually refers to those little beach stands that serve drinks, food or, both either seasonally or year-round. In Málaga, some of the beachfront chiringuitos are actually full restaurants that operate all year. The views and relaxed atmosphere in these places are sometimes just what the soul needs. Simply take a stroll down the beachfront walk and go for one that pulls you! One chiringuito, however, that has changed up the typical beach fare and decoration is Frida Pahlo (located in the historical fishing neighborhood of El Palo…get it?). As the name would suggest, it is more like fusion cuisine with a heavy Mexican influence. They also have a lovely terrace on which to enjoy some tasty cocktails!

20. LITTLE GEMS

Quality. Service. Flavor. These are just a few of the words used to describe La Casa del Perro, one of Málaga´s little hidden gems. This unpretentious place with a bright blue exterior is actually a bit hard to find but seek it out because it has the quality trifecta that makes it worth a visit. First, the owners´ welcoming and warm relationship with their customers makes you feel right at home; second, the menu is unique and varied according to seasonal produce; and third, it´s truly homemade like a Spanish grandmother would make only much more modern and sassy. Oh, and they serve natural wine, too! If you have a yen for international dishes, hop to and grab a table at Mamuchis in the Soho district. Serving up homemade Greek, Indonesian, and Mexican dishes with attentive service and a unique decorative atmosphere is their strong suit. Be sure to make reservations because these are small venues.

21. TOURISTY HAVENS

So you show up here in your Ray Bans with the idea of eating like a local. You are a tourist but you don´t wanna seem like one. In theory, you walk down to the popular "Muelle 1" area (the port area) trying to shun the places that are packed with nordic types that look like boiled lobsters next to the locals. Well, it´s pretty impossible to not be sucked into the tourist ambiance so you decide to just embrace the abundance that the very tourist industry affords. One place worthy of embrace is Casa Lola. You´ll see lines of people forming to get into this place even though there are several of them in the center. I was once with a friend on the terrace of Pez Lola carrying on a fluent Spanish conversation and I swear, the tourists were looking at us like WE were the outsiders!

22. CHEAP EATS

It wouldn't be right if there wasn't any mention of economic eateries in this guide. My objective is to suggest places where you'll have an optimal experience but sometimes a menu on a budget is the way it's gotta be. In this case, I'd point you to a fixture in Spain called 100 Montaditos. It could work for you if: 1) you have blown all your dough on travel and lodging; or 2) your adventures have made you so light and carefree you feel like a young college student again (or you actually are a college student!). Indeed, this is a place where young folks go to have a cheap bite, a beer and, of course, some social stimulation. But even older folks enjoy this sort of vibe. What are montaditos? To put it briefly, they are like fast food tapas. Mini sandwiches on baguette bread with dozens of fillings like hot dog, burger, chicken, tuna, cheese or even Spanish tortilla inside. The expense-saving and efficient service routine requires you to tick what you want and write your name on an order sheet at your table, then pay at the bar and pick up when ready.

23. GET YOUR HEALTHY ON!

Any of you out there with food restrictions or allergies that prohibit too much reliance on restaurant food loaded with wheat, eggs, and milk products? Hey, me too! When visiting any unfamiliar place, I always like to have an eye out for a great place to get something light or as a meal replacement for the days when I just need a break. Luckily there are some places in Málaga offering healthful smoothies and juices to "mimar" or pamper your tummy. Try Reviv in the center where they offer lovely juices and smoothies and some original cakes and truffles. El Último Mono is a great place for coffee as well as vitamin-packed juices and smoothies.

24. FANCY SCHMANCY

If you´re looking to spend a little more for a truly unique fine dining experience, Málaga boasts a plethora of restaurants that serve more elaborate creations designed and prepared by top chefs. La Antxoeta Art Restaurant comes highly recommended for both quality ingredients and excellent service. The ambiance is pleasing but with cozier proportions so you´ll need to make reservations. Located on the side of Mount Gibralfaro overlooking the Paseo del Parque and the port, Mi Niña Lola is the best place to try unique concept food with a spectacular view. The young chefs at MNL combine Malagueñan recipes with international flavors that make up the multi-cultural landscape of Málaga. The idea here is to order more dishes that are smaller in size, 4 to 5 per person, in order to experience a wider variety of taste sensations.

Eat Like a Local

25. NO MEAT? NO PROBLEM!

If you are not into eating meat or animal products it won´t be difficult to find restaurants that have vegetarian and vegan options. There are quite a few traditional tapas that don´t involve meat, but perhaps leaving out the eggs and dairy as well will make it a little more complicated. Nonetheless, there are a few healthy recommendations that are worth a visit. While not a vegan restaurant, Noviembre has great salads and you can create your own salad, sandwich or burger to your liking. MIMO Vegan Bistro is like gourmet for vegans! They also use seasonal, organic produce with gluten-free options as well.

26. MÁLAGA MULTI-CULTI

You can see the blending of two distinct cultures everywhere you look in this city. Within a cozy distance you have both the Alcazaba, an Arabic fortress built after the North African Moors invaded in 711 A.D., and the impressive Catedral de la Encarnación, built to glorify the Christian defeat and expulsion of the Moors some 800 years later. Though these stunning constructions might represent the cultural conflicts of the past, in our modern times they seem to represent peaceful co-existence and mutual respect. Now different cultural groups represent their culture through cuisine and we all benefit from that! Yum! For an international dining experience, I can recommend La Pachamama. They serve Peruvian treats like ceviche and a variety of seafood and meat dishes. Try the pisco sour if you're in the mood for a cocktail! Gastrobar Andino serves an intriguing mix of Latin American dishes from various countries like Bolivia, Colombia, and Venezuela.

27. MEXICAN HAT DANCE

Mexican food fans unite! There´s always gonna be a "mono" (literally "monkey," figuratively "craving") for Mexican food sooner or later. If you get one of those monkeys on your back while visiting Málaga, you´re in luck! Cantina Niña Bonita is a must-try serving non-GMO corn tortillas made in-house along with the salsas. Often lauded as the best Mexican restaurant in Málaga, you´ll find tasty, homemade Mexican dishes all gluten-free. Walking by Tulum, you´ll be pulled into their tiny dining room with a sense that there´s something good waiting. Homemade margaritas and slowly marinated pulled pork tacos enjoyed in their cozy upstairs dining room is the best!

28. FROM THE FAR EAST

If you´re not an Asian food fan you can just skip this tip. Me? I am a huge Asian food fan! If I can´t find a really good Chinese, Japanese, or Thai restaurant in my town, I go to the extra trouble of finding all the ingredients to cook my own authentic Asian dishes at home. Luckily, there are some keepers here that caught my attention for their quality, variety, and presentation. For a lovely ambiance and exquisite sushi creations, visit Haruki. Uri Sushi, which has both Japanese and Korean dishes, is about the size of a walk-in closet but the quality is amazing. Lastly, Woococo seems to be something of an undiscovered gem of Korean cooking. Word on the street is the dishes are the closest you´ll get to authentic Korean in Málaga.

29. DOLCE VITTORIA

At the risk of being rejected for its location in a very touristy street in Málaga, the Pizzería Italiana Vittoria has earned its stripes when it comes to excellent food and service. They have all the usual favorites plus a few original pastas and pizzas of their own. The dessert menu includes a few typical Italian "dolces" like tiramisu and torta de la nonna. The Nutella cheesecake is "delizioso" (said with an emphatic gesture of three fingertips to the lips and a kissing sound) and all of the desserts are homemade.
One thing that grabbed my attention was the very Italian wine list with several reds, whites, a rosé or two, and even a few proseccos.

30. STREET FOOD

If you don´t know what an "empanada" is, it´s a bread-like or crust-like dough, filled with meat or vegetarian fillings and baked into a half-moon shape. You can easily buy and eat these as you´re walking along the street, or take some home for later. El Ombú has some of the best Argentinian empanadas in town. They have several vegetarian options along with the more traditional spicy meat, chicken, and tuna ones. I actually really love the crusty-textured empanadas with "pisto," a tasty tomato sauce filling, from a local grocery store chain called Dia.

Eat Like a Local

31. LATE NIGHT EATS

Quick, cheap, late-night food - the best prescription after you've gone a little OTT (over the top) in your vacational revelry. A few common offerings are the traditional Malagueño sandwich, the "campero," which is made on round, fluffy bread called "mollete" and filled with normal sandwich fillings. You can also opt for a Turkish-style pita sandwich called "kebap." These are made from those big logs of meat that turn vertically while roasting on a skewer...not the most attractive sight. But when you're a sight for sore eyes, only the taste really matters plus these babies will really soak up the alcohol. A La Turca Halal on the Plaza de la Merced is open until 2:00 am Sunday through Thursday and until 3:00 am on Friday and Saturday.

32. ITALY'S GOT NOTHING ON US!

The "gelato" of Italy may be world-famous, but here in Spain, the "helado" (pronounced el-AH-do) gives gelato a run for its money. Not only is it basically the same texture and appearance, but it is also super yummy! There are a few "heladerías" that come highly recommended in Málaga including Casa Mira, which is probably the most well-known and is apparently the official ice cream supplier of the Spanish royal family! Also, check out Yummy right up the street from the cathedral which has a selection of regular and vegan ice creams that are truly delish. I am always impressed with the texture and flavor of the vegan helados, just like the real thing! Look for their unique flavors like pumpkin coconut and mascarpone with cherries and white chocolate.

33. THANK YOU, SPANIARDS, FOR THE CHOCOLATE

We should really thank the Mayan civilization and the Spider Monkeys of the South American rainforests for giving us the materia prima for chocolate. However, according to those at the Mayan Monkey Chocolate Factory and Museum in Mijas, the Spaniards also played an essential role in the diffusion of chocolate throughout the world. They first brought cacao to Spain through the ports of Andalusia where it gradually spread up into the rest of European society. If you're up for a trip that's a little out of the way, you can visit the Mayan Monkey in Mijas Pueblo about 30 km down the coast to the west where they offer homemade ice cream and artisan chocolate. Both kids and adults can also take part in chocolate-making workshops.

34. COCKTAILS AL FRESCO WITH A BIRD'S EYE VIEW

Did you know that Málaga boasts around 300 sunny days on average per year? Having come from rainy Asturias, I was amazed at how many buildings both public and private have a rooftop terrace built right in. I live on the 4th floor of my building (which has a terrace) and I can see the terraces of all the private residences and hotels around me. Málaga is rooftop terrace obsessed and that means you can enjoy cocktails with a view of Málaga's beautiful sunsets! Here are just a few popular rooftop bars to try: AC Hotel Málaga Palacio, Room Mate Larios Hotel, and Mariposa Hotel Roof Terrace.

35. MÁLAGA WINE

Me before coming to Spain: "Uh, no idea about wine." Me after coming to Spain: "Oh ya, that's a good varietal, I really love the reds from Toro and blah blah blah...". Once I realized that enjoying a good wine was affordable and available to everyone in Spain, I naturally started to taste, experiment, and learn about the different wine regions, grapes and flavors involved. If the wine world has piqued your interest as well, why not try (and learn about) some great local wines? Check out Anyway Wine Bar where they have an excellent selection of whites, reds, rosés, sweet wines, and more. They have many wines from Málaga province and other regions of Spain accompanied by a menu of cured meats and cheeses to contrast your palate for the best experience.

36. THE WEEKEND RITUAL OF VERMOUTH

The phrase "la hora de vermút" is something you will commonly hear around 1 pm on a Sunday in Málaga and many other parts of Spain. If you´re not familiar, vermouth is a wine-based apéritif that is flavored with herbs and spices. Having a pre-lunch vermouth with a few tapas is not a new practice in this part of the world and, even though it was new to me, I immediately embraced this ritual! Try and get out a bit early for the vermouth hour because the bars and "vermuterías" will certainly be packed by 1:30 pm. As with wine, you can order many brands of vermouth from a bottle but in the most popular establishments, try to get "vermút de barril" or from the barrel. Ask for a local one in any case! La Tranca is always a hit with foreigners, and La Pachá is a tiny little corner taberna that couldn´t be more Malagueño.

37. CREATIVE COCKTAILERY

There is no lack of places to order cocktails in Málaga. But you'll want to ratchet up the enjoyment factor of your stay to the max, so why not try something a bit more…original? La Valiente Gastrobar is the place to go and I'll tell you why. Their mission is, in their own words, "the search for creative freedom through dishes, cocktails, and wines." Apart from the tasty tapas offerings, they have quite a long list of signature cocktails with names like, "Love Lavanda," "Moon Collins," and "Electrica." If alcohol is a no-can-do for you, there's a selection of mocktails as well.

38. WHERE EVERYBODY KNOWS YOUR NAME

Well, maybe they don´t know your name…mine either. But the Antigua Casa de Guardia is just the place for the clinking of glasses with a hearty, "Cheers!". This old-fashioned tavern founded in 1840, is a perfect example of "solera" (see Tip 40). Tradition and a sense of history abound amidst the two-hundred-year-old barrels full of Málagueño sweet wines, not to mention the old practice of scribbling your drink tab directly on the bar top in chalk. Among this amazing local selection of wines, you´ll find one called "Her Majesty Isabel II," (Queen Elizabeth II of Great Britain) which has been aged for 7 years. It seems the founder, Don José de la Guardia, had something of a friendship with the British monarch! Whichever wine you choose, there are also seafood tapas you can enjoy alongside your royal "vino".

39. THE ALCHEMY OF WINE

If you are a wine lover, you´ll appreciate knowing the word "maridaje". This refers to the art (and science) of combining the right wines with the right foods by taking into account the richness, acidity, and intensity to create harmony between the food and drink. In other words, the "maridaje" is the search for the alchemy of the perfect flavor. If this doesn´t make you want to reserve a table at the Vinoteca Los Patios de Beatas where their sommeliers will help you match the perfect wines with your selected dishes, I don´t know what will! There you will find a feast for the senses including stained glass windows in a beautifully remodeled palatial home from the 18th century.

40. A TASTE OF HISTORY

Perhaps you´ve noticed that many places you see in Málaga have a quality that feels like a deep rootedness or a strong sense of legacy. Locals call this "solera." This term refers to a sense of tradition and valued customs that have become instilled in the daily life and culture of a people. If you´re looking for a truly local experience, stop by one of Málaga´s old-time delicatessens. With almost 100 years of offering high-quality local products, La Mallorquina represents the sense of "solera" at its best. Located on the beautiful Plaza Félix Sáenz, you can buy excellent ham, salt cod, wines, cheese, preserves, and other staples. You can also get bakery goods from the La Mallorquina "panadería" right next door.

41. AUTHENTIC MARKET ATMOSPHERE

On my first visit to Málaga several years ago, I was really drawn to the Mercado de Atarazanas. The name "atarazanas" comes from Arabic and literally means "place where ships are built." The striking arch at the front of the building would have been one of seven such arches in the original "atarazanas" or shipyards built under the Muslim rulers of the 14th century. Nowadays it´s a fresh food market buzzing with activity from 8:00 am to 3:00 pm Monday through Saturday. Come and peruse the eye-catching displays of dried fruits and nuts, olives, fresh seafood, fish, meat, and produce. I´ve found the quality of products to be high and prices reasonable. After shopping, you can take advantage of the fresh seafood tapas available at the Bar Mercado Atarazanas.

42. THE ENGLISH CUT

If you haven't yet been to the "El Corte Inglés" store, you've simply gotta go just for the shopping! It is the Harrod's of Spain which means it is a very well-respected and trusted establishment. Málaga's "El Corte Inglés" has 7 floors most of which are dedicated to high-quality clothes, designer fashion, shoes, cosmetics, accessories, and the like. So why is it in this guide? Because "El Corte Inglés" also has a reputable supermarket that usually has what you cannot find in other places. They also have a gourmet shop and food court called "El Gourmet Experience" on the top floor. The best part, however, is the amazing panoramic view from the rooftop terrace where you can sip your "café" and maybe snap a few photos. All this from a humble tailor's shop that began in Madrid in the year 1890!

43. IF YOUR BLOOD RUNS GREEN

Easy access to good EVOO, extra virgin olive oil, is one of the gifts of Spain that I don´t take for granted. This green, viscous elixir is one of the best oils that you can use both for its zesty flavor and well-documented health benefits. Just a few drops of this stuff and all your tastebuds are immersed in that peppery, pungent hit that tells you that it´s packed with antioxidants and more. Luckily for you, Andalusia happens to be one of the biggest producers of olive oil in the world. Take advantage of your stay in this olive haven to do a tasting or even visit an olive farm where you can see the process of production in action. If you´re just looking to take some home, visit the old delicatessen shops like La Mallorquina or Zoilo which carry only the best quality olive oils.

44. A PINCH OF SPICE IN PARADISE

Leave some extra room in your backpack when you're packing for your return trip because you'll want to take home some exotic spices and aromatic teas from La Tienda de las Especias located on the Pasillo Santa Isabel. This is yet another place in Málaga that feels as if you've been beamed into the past. They have everything from pink peppercorns to Ras al Hanout. Be prepared to ask for quantities in grams as much of it is in bulk, although some items may come in little packets. For the home chef who is a fan of international flavors, it's like a kid in a candy shop! Part of the shop is dedicated to La Boutique del Té so you can also get some wonderful aromatic whole leaf teas as well.

45. APERITIF, ANYONE?

For me, this word conjures the image of a classy little drink in hand while one works the room at a party. Although the word "aperitivo" in Spanish can refer to drinks taken before a meal, the term often makes reference to the salty foods that accompany drinks. If you peer into the window of a shop selling "aperitivos," you'll see a variety of dried fruit and nuts, artisan potato chips, and sweets. How very old-fashioned European! Go and see for yourself at Patatas Paco José which abounds with shelves of roasted nuts and dried fruit along with a big vat of potato chips. At Christmas time the striking storefront is a sight to behold decorated with fairy lights, garlands, and candy canes.

46. FESTIVAL FOOD

I hope you get to experience Easter Week in Málaga at least once in your life. During this time, known locally as "Semana Santa", you'll witness countless processions where hundreds of men carry heavy platforms with sacred religious images known as "tronos." You don't have to be Catholic or even religious to be moved by these solemn and lengthy marches which happen all around the city. Some Easter Week goodies to be on the lookout for are "torrijas," "pestiños," and "buñuelos." Torrijas are very similar to French toast but sweeter when soaked in honey. Pestiños are pieces of fried dough dipped in spiced honey and aniseed. Buñuelos are doughnut-like balls fried and rolled in sugar. For something savory, try cod croquettes.

47. CHESTNUTS A´ ROASTING

In Montana, USA there are no chestnut trees. I could only listen to the festive songs about roasting chestnuts over an open fire, and that sounded romantic to me. But I had no idea that once autumn arrived in northern Spain, I would be able to stop at roasted chestnut "kiosks" where there´d be a señora with her roaster fired up and sheets of newspaper rolled into cone shapes. Those warm chestnuts in a paper cone are the quintessence of autumn and they are a tradition in Spain. Here in Málaga, I was even more surprised to see they are cooked in a traditional way with enamel pots placed over a fire in a tin drum. The season starts in October and goes through November. Just follow the smoke signals!

48. FOOD FAIRS WITH FLAIR

Fiestas gastronómicas are very common in every part of Spain. A food festival is always a very local affair because the featured food is always something particular to that area, something traditional and well-loved by the inhabitants that they´ve been making or harvesting with pride for centuries. When I lived in Asturias, some of the local festivals were around "fabada," a hearty Asturian bean stew, "setas," mushrooms that grew easily in the wet climate, and "mejillones," mussels and other fruits of the sea. Here in the south of Spain, the products are quite different. In the first week of August, visitors and locals alike can look forward to the "Fiesta del Gazpacho" in Alfarnatejo, a mountain village northeast of Málaga City. On the second Sunday of September, they celebrate the "Fiesta del Boquerón Victoriana" (a fresh anchovy-like blue fish) in Rincon de la Victoria, only a short hop to the east of Málaga city. On the first weekend of October, you can attend the "Feria del Queso Artesanal" (artisan cheese fair) en Teba, a little town in the hills northeast of Málaga city. Attend one of these and you´ll really feel like a local. These are just a few to stoke your curiosity.

49. CHRISTMAS TIME, OH CHRISTMAS TIME

Turrón (pronounced "too-RONE") is probably the best-known and loved sweet at Christmas all over Spain. This is no less true in Málaga. Though typically almond-based, these rectangle-shaped bars come in so many different versions including chocolate, coconut, yogurt, nuts, and fruit. Also, be on the lookout for "roscos de vino," donut-shaped cookies with a soft, crumbly texture. My favorite festive sweet is the "Roscón de Reyes" which is eaten to celebrate the Magi Kings Day on January 6th. Found in every corner bakery and supermarket, these large ring-shaped pastries showcase dried fruit and a filling of chocolate or vanilla whipped cream, or pastry cream. A tiny plastic figurine is baked inside; if you find it in your piece, you will have good luck for the new year. If you want just a slice of "roscón" with your coffee, head to Lepanto Café on Calle Larios.

50. EL PIMPI LEGACY

I could not possibly offer up a food guide about Málaga without mentioning the ever-popular Bar Bodega El Pimpi smack in the center of Málaga. I think you'll agree that this is a place with "encanto." Although it's something of a mecca for tourists, the roots of El Pimpi run much deeper into the heart of Málaga through its support of culture, traditions, and the arts. It doesn't hurt that the place is associated with many celebrity names who have passed through its doors, not least of which is famous local resident and partner in the enterprise, Antonio Banderas. In fact, Mr. Banderas has shot scenes from one of his movies within these walls. I quite like the indoor ambiance among the barrels of wine but the outdoor terrace is equally enchanting with its view of an 11th-century Moorish fortress. This singular spot is the place to enjoy some traditional Málagueño dishes while gazing at the tawny glow of the fading sunset reflecting off of the Alcazaba. Ahhh….Málaga.

OTHER RESOURCES:

The Guide to Málaga is a great resource for your next trip to Málaga! It covers not only food, but what to do, what to see, events, and much more!

www.guidetomalaga.com

READ OTHER BOOKS BY CZYK PUBLISHING

Eat Like a Local United States Cities & Towns

Eat Like a Local United States

Eat Like a Local- Oklahoma: Oklahoma Food Guide

Eat Like a Local- North Carolina: North Carolina Food Guide

Eat Like a Local- New York City: New York City Food Guide

Children's Book: Charlie the Cavalier Travels the World by Lisa Rusczyk

Eat Like a Local

Follow *Eat Like a Local* on Amazon.
Join our mailing list for new books

http://bit.ly/EatLikeaLocalbooks

CZYKPublishing.com

Printed in Great Britain
by Amazon